KU-192-747

Some sixty million years ago America and Siberia were joined by a land bridge, almost a thousand miles wide, where they are now separated by the Bering Strait. Across this bridge mammals entered America from Asia and Europe. The land bridge then became submerged, and it was not until about a million years ago that the succession of Ice Ages caused the sea level to fall, and re-opened the bridge.

Many species must have disappeared during the Ice Ages, but Siberia, Alaska and part of Canada were not covered by ice, and the migrations of animals were resumed. These conditions lasted until about twelve thousand years ago, when the land bridge again disappeared.

In addition to this, the land bridge between North and South America was established only a few million years ago. Until then, Central America was a group of large islands, but with the emergence of the land bridge, the fauna of South America had access to North America. Thus, the mammals of North America are made up of the remnants of the original fauna, such as the Pronghorn and Prairie Dog, of immigrants from Asia such as the Weasels, Bison and Wolf, and immigrants from South America such as the Porcupine and Opossum.

Some species, of course, failed to cross the land bridge — or to survive if they did. In North America there are no Apes or Monkeys, no Giraffes, no Civets or Mongooses. But this enormous continent, stretching from the Arctic to the North Tropic Region, contains mammals of great variety and interest. Let us hope that this will always be so.

A Ladybird Book
Series 691

'North American Mammals' is the third in a series of Ladybird books about animals of the world.

John Leigh-Pemberton's superb full-colour illustrations are supported by an informative text about the mammals of great variety and interest which are contained in that enormous continent stretching from the Arctic to the North Tropic Region.

A coloured chart shows the various types of habitat of these mammals. An index is given and also - at the back - the various Orders and Families to which they belong.

NORTH AMERICAN MAMMALS

written and illustrated by
JOHN LEIGH-PEMBERTON

Publishers: Wills & Hepworth Ltd., Loughborough

First published 1970 *Printed in England*

Canadian Porcupine *(above)*

Length, head and body	70 cm.
Length of tail	22 cm.

Alaskan Pika *(below)*

Length, head and body	20 cm.
	(Average)

Porcupines are Rodents, belonging in America to the family *Erithizontidae,* and are found in wooded areas from Alaska to Mexico. Mainly nocturnal, they live in caves or in hollow logs.

Once a year a single offspring is born, with eyes open and weighing about 1·5 kg.—more than a newly born Black Bear cub. It is equipped with soft 2 cm. quills which rapidly harden after birth.

Adult Porcupines have about thirty thousand 5 cm. needle sharp quills which they can erect if in danger. These become easily detached from the skin and impale themselves in an adversary's flesh.

Porcupines climb well and will sit for days at a time in one tree, eating the bark which is their principal item of diet.

The mammalian order *Lagomorpha* contains two families, the *Ochotonidae* (Pikas or Conies), and the *Leporidae* (the Hares and Rabbits).

The two North American species of Pika are small, tailless animals living in communities among rocks. They are diurnal (active in daytime) and inhabit mountainous country from Alaska to California. In spite of the severe winter climate of the northern part of their range, they do not hibernate. They are vegetarian, and are remarkable for the way in which they make 'hay' from vegetable matter. This they cut and dry, repeatedly moving it to keep it in the sun. It is then stored in hollow 'haystacks' beneath overhanging rocks for winter use.

Pikas, sometimes known as Whistling Hares, utter high-pitched cries. They breed as often as three times a year, producing from two to six young at a time.

4

0 7214 0272 0

| **American Marten** | Length, head and body | 50 cm. |
| (above) | Length of tail | 25 cm. |

| **Snowshoe Hare** | Length, head and body | 48 cm. |
| (below) | Length of tail | 5 cm. |

Many members of the *Mustelidae* family are found in North America. These are the Weasels, Minks, Martens and Skunks—carnivores which have been much hunted for their beautiful fur.

The American Marten lives principally in Canadian forests, where it preys on Squirrels, hunting by day and night. It also catches birds and rabbits and, like other members of its family, has a great liking for fruit.

One to four young are born each year. They are fully grown in about three months.

There are eighteen species of Hares and Rabbits *(Leporidae)* in North America—more than anywhere else in the world. Broadly speaking, rabbits are those members of the family which live in burrows and produce litters of blind, naked and somewhat immature young. Hares live above ground, and their leverets—as the young are called—are kept in a 'form' or nest. At birth they are fully furred and have open eyes, and they are very soon independent of their mother.

The Snowshoe Hare, so named because of its large, furred feet, lives in evergreen forest areas from northern Canada to central California. The summer coat is gray, but in the northern part of its range it changes to white in winter. Two litters a year, of three or four young, are normal, but in years of 'population explosion' (which occur from time to time) there may be four litters, with as many as eight in each.

Hares feed on vegetation at dawn and dusk. They are a principal source of food to many predators, leverets being especially vulnerable.

Prairie Dog *(above)*	Length, head and body	30 cm.
	Length of tail	8 cm.
Cottontail Rabbit *(below)*	Length of head and body	38 cm.
	Length of tail	5 cm.
	(Size varies according to species).	

Prairie Dogs are Rodents, members of the Squirrel family *(Sciuridae)*, of which there are many species in North America. They are now much rarer than they used to be. They inhabit open prairies where they build complex and extensive burrow systems. These burrows are constructed with a domed entrance to prevent flooding from heavy rain. Burrow systems are large—like 'towns'—with populations of thousands, and with a definite social order by which the community is regulated. Sentries are posted to keep watch for predators such as Hawks, Snakes and Badgers, and barking alarm cries are uttered if danger threatens.

From two to ten young are born once a year. They are fully grown in fifteen months. Grass forms the principal food, and Prairie Dogs do much damage to pasture land.

The Cottontail Rabbit, of which there are about thirteen species, is another member of the family *Leporidae*. They occupy various habitats from southern Canada to Argentina, and range in size from the little Brush Rabbit of the arid plains to the large Swamp Rabbit of the lower Mississippi River basin.

Cottontails live in burrows but, except for the Brush Rabbit, do not dig them themselves. From three to five litters are produced every year, averaging four young in each litter. The young are placed in a nest above ground and, with the exception of the Swamp Rabbit, are born blind, naked and helpless. Curiously, Cottontails very rarely survive in captivity.

This is one of the most abundant mammals in North America, and is an important source of food for man as well as for predators.

North American Flying Squirrel *(above)*	Length of head and body	24 cm.
	Length of tail	15 cm.
American Mink *(below)*	Length of head and body	40 cm.
	Length of tail	18 cm.

North American Flying Squirrels (family *Sciuridae*) are found in wooded areas from southern Alaska to Utah and California. A flattened tail and panels of loose skin, stretched between front and hind legs, enable them to glide rather than 'fly' from tree to tree. They are nocturnal and live mostly on acorns and nuts, but will also eat meat and insects.

Hollow trees, or the holes made by Woodpeckers, provide them with nests, and in cold weather several dozen will congregate in one nest for warmth. They will also invade houses or take over the nesting boxes of birds.

From two to six young are born in one litter, and they are blind, naked and weigh only two or three grams at birth. The young do not develop as quickly as other Rodents, and are about seventy days old before they attempt to glide.

Mink are Carnivores, belonging to the family *Mustelidae*. They inhabit wooded areas with streams or rivers and are equally at home on land or in water. Waterfowl, fish and frogs are caught in the water, and Mink can swim underwater and dive to a considerable depth. On land, birds and mammals as large as a rabbit are taken.

Mink are solitary animals, living in holes in river banks, in tree stumps or in the nests of other animals. From four to ten young are born at a time, and female Mink are particularly good mothers. They can hiss and scream in anger and, like some other members of this family, emit a terrible odour from scent glands.

Mink are found throughout the United States and most of Canada.

| **Eastern Chipmunk** (above) | Length, head and body | 16 cm. |
| | Length of tail | 10 cm. |

| **White-footed Mouse** (below) | Length, head and body | 10 cm. |
| | Length of tail | 10 cm. |

Many of the North American members of the family *Sciuridae* are ground-living Squirrels, such as the Marmots, Ground Squirrels and Chipmunks. They inhabit forested areas, prairies or mountains. All live in burrows, either natural cavities or systems constructed by themselves, and all are vegetarian—with some insect food; a few species are semi-carnivorous.

Chipmunks are plentiful in south-eastern Canada and in the eastern United States. One or two litters of four or five young are born each year. Like other members of this family, Chipmunks have delicate little hands with which they collect their food and stuff it into special dry pouches within the mouth. Some food is stored for the winter, when partial hibernation takes place.

White-footed Mice, or Deer Mice, are found all over America as far north as Labrador. They occupy almost any sort of habitat and are very abundant. As many as four litters a year, containing five young, are quite normal and these mice begin to breed at seven weeks old. They make nests lined with vegetable down in small burrows or crevices, and a new nest is made as soon as the old one becomes dirty.

Although belonging to a different family *(Cricetidae)* and genus *(Peromyscus)* they are very similar to the Field Mouse *(Muridae)* of the Old World.

White-footed Mice are said to 'sing'. They certainly utter a series of high-pitched squeaks and also 'drum' with their front feet. The diet is very varied, including seeds and fruit as well as insects and carrion.

Fox Squirrels *(above)*	*Length, head and body*	*36 cm.*
	Length of tail	*26 cm.*
Eastern Gray Fox	*Length, head and body*	*60 cm.*
(below)	*Length of tail*	*40 cm.*

There are about fifty species of Tree Squirrels *(Sciuridae)* in the world and they are found in Europe, Asia, Japan and in North and South America. Of these, the Fox Squirrels of the eastern United States occur in various forms and in a puzzling variety of colours. Many have orange or red bellies, some have white noses and ears, and melanism—the tendency to be very dark or black—in common.

Fox Squirrels are slightly bigger than the Eastern Gray Squirrels which have been introduced into Britain. They are diurnal and arboreal, living on nuts, acorns, birds' eggs and some insects. In winter they build nests in cavities in hollow trees, which they adapt to a suitable size, but summer nests, or 'dreys', are built in the branches. New nests are built as soon as old ones become fouled or infested with fleas. Three or four young are born in each litter, and older squirrels produce two litters a year.

North America has three species of Fox: the Red Fox, similar to that of Europe and Asia; the small, rather rare Kit Fox, and the Gray Fox which ranges from southern Canada to northern South America.

Gray Foxes live in wooded areas or in rocky country. They do not dig 'earths' but live in natural cavities, particularly in hollow trees. These they will quite readily climb—an unusual activity for the family *Canidae*. They are also less carnivorous than other Foxes, much of their diet consisting of grass, fruit and nuts.

Three or four cubs are born in one litter each year.

Beaver *(above)*	*Length, head and body*	*100 cm.* ⎫ *Average*
	Length of tail	*30 cm.* ⎭
Musk Rat *(below)*	*Length, head and body*	*30 cm.*
	Length of tail	*25 cm.*

Beavers are Rodents, members of the family *Castoridae*. They are found only in North America and in a few places in Europe. These large aquatic animals are fully adapted to the life they lead; they have webbed hind feet, a tail like a paddle, and teeth like chisels which can gnaw through most trees.

Their food consists of the bark and leaves of such trees as willow, alder and birch. The usual number of young in a litter is two to four, born furred and with eyes open.

Most Beavers live in lodges—hollow piles of sticks, stones and mud some 1·5 metres high. These have an underwater entrance, and in order to keep the necessary level of water, Beavers create ponds by building dams across the stream. These are made by felling trees and pushing them into position with mud and other vegetation to bind and anchor them. Short canals are made into woodland in order to launch these logs, the bark of which is used for winter feeding.

Beavers work co-operatively in keeping lodge and dam in repair, and they usually live in family parties. They have been continuously hunted for their beautiful fur and, although now increasing in numbers, were once very rare.

Another aquatic Rodent is the Musk Rat (family *Cricetidae*), found throughout most of Canada and in the United States. Musk Rats occupy burrows in the banks of streams, or create 'houses' in marshland.

The fur known as 'Musquash' is derived from this animal. Several litters of five or seven young are produced annually.

| **Fisher** *(above)* | Length, head and body | 56 cm. |
| | Length of tail | 40 cm. |

| **Striped Skunk** *(below)* | Length, head and body | 35 cm. |
| | Length of tail | 40 cm. |

Many of the North American *Mustelidae* have superb fur, for which they have been hunted. As a result, some species have been almost exterminated, and only recently—as a result of enforced protection—have they recovered in numbers. An example is the Fisher, a large Marten found in wooded areas from Canada to New England and New York State.

Fishers spend more time on the ground than other Martens, and their food consists of larger prey such as Snowshoe Hares and Porcupines. Even Deer are also eaten.

Between one and five (usually four) young are born in a litter, and the family requires a large range of territory. In spite of their name, they do not necessarily eat more fish than other Martens.

Skunks are also members of the family *Mustelidae,* and in North America there are four species—the Striped Skunk (shown here, and the commonest), the Hooded Skunk, the Spotted Skunk and the Hog-nosed Skunk. They occupy a variety of habitats from woodland to desert, and all produce from two to five young.

Skunks make dens in burrows or rock cavities and are principally nocturnal. Their food consists of many insects (including bees), small rodents and some vegetation.

When frightened or annoyed, a Skunk turns its back on an enemy, sometimes stands on its hands, erects its tail and emits from special glands a jet of liquid. This not only has the most appalling smell, but also burns the skin and eyes. Even the largest and hungriest predators respect the Skunk and avoid it.

18

| **Douglas Squirrel (Chickaree)** *(above)* | Length, head and body | 18 cm. |
| | Length of tail | 12 cm. |

| **Cacomistle (Ring-tailed Cat)** *(below)* | Length, head and body | 35 cm. |
| | Length of tail | 37 cm. |

American Red Squirrels (family *Sciuridae*) are placed in a separate genus *(Tamiasciurus)* by themselves. There are two species, the Eastern Red Squirrel and the Douglas Squirrel which is found on the Pacific side of North America from British Columbia to California. These very attractive little animals inhabit pine forest or woodland where seed-bearing trees abound, and live on pine cones, acorns, young birds and birds' eggs. They are active in daylight and sometimes at night.

Litters usually consist of four young, born in a nest which is usually in a tree cavity.

Chickarees are quiet creatures in the spring, but become very bold and noisy in autumn. They are much preyed on by Martens, Foxes and Weasels.

The family *Procyonidae* contains the Raccoons, Pandas, Coatis and the interesting little Cacomistle, which is found from Oregon, through Texas to Mexico. It inhabits rocky areas, usually near water or woodland, and it is a good climber. This is really a nocturnal animal and is omnivorous, although at some times of the year it is almost entirely insectivorous.

Cacomistles live in hollow trees or in holes among rocks. Here the female makes a den and produces three or four young. At birth these are covered with fine white hair, but at four months old are similar to their parents.

Cacomistles make excellent pets and early settlers in America kept them as mousers, at which they are most efficient. In spite of their nick-name of 'Ring-tailed Cat', they are, of course, no relation to the Cat *(Felidae)* family, but they are placed in the order *Carnivora*.

Raccoon *(above)*	Length, head and body	55 cm.
	Length of tail	40 cm.
Opossum *(below)*	Length, head and body	45 cm.
	Length of tail	40 cm.

Of the seven species of Raccoon (family *Procyonidae*), only one is found in North America, inhabiting woodland areas from southern Canada to central America. Mostly nocturnal, they live in hollow trees or among rocks, and in the northern part of their range they go into partial winter hibernation.

Raccoons are usually solitary and are omnivorous, but they particularly favour such food as frogs and fish and are, therefore, usually found near water. Most food is washed before being eaten, and this is especially so in the case of Raccoons in captivity. There are three or four young in a litter.

Sensitive noses and delicate hands give Raccoons a highly-developed sense of touch. They climb and swim well and, for their size, are among the animal world's most efficient fighters.

The order *Marsupialia is fairly well represented in South America, but in North America only one species, the American Opossum (family *Didelphidae*) is found. These primitive but tough mammals have managed to survive in spite of predators and persecution, and are found chiefly in forest areas, usually near water, from southern Canada to central America. They are nocturnal and omnivorous, and make grass nests in cavities or burrows. Partial hibernation takes place in the northern part of the range, but only for spells of really cold weather.

One litter of up to eighteen young (of which only seven survive) is born each year, after a gestation period of only thirteen days. As with all marsupials, the young are minute and immature, spending their first two months in the mother's fur-lined pouch.

* *Marsupials are discussed at greater length in 'Australian Mammals' in this series.*

Grizzly Bear

Length, head and body	250 cm.
Shoulder height	150 cm.
Weight	400 kg.

Grizzly Bears are generally regarded as being of the same species as the Brown Bears of Europe and Asia. They are, however, a great deal bigger and, in fact, the Alaskan Brown Bears (a sub-species) are the largest land carnivores in the world.

Grizzlies (family *Ursidae*) were once spread over much of Canada, Alaska and the United States as far south as Mexico, but they are now very rare in the United States except in National Parks, and are usually found in the wild only in Canada and Alaska.

Like other Bears they are omnivorous, preying on Bison and cattle, as well as eating plant food and catching salmon. Grizzlies do not usually attack human beings unless provoked or startled. They are said not to like the taste of human flesh, but—like most Bears—they are very inquisitive and temperamentally unreliable, and therefore can be dangerous. Apart from Man they have few enemies, and are able to despatch any adversary with blows from their powerful fore-paws.

They sleep through the winter, but it is not true hibernation as their pulse rate and temperature do not alter. During this period spent in a den, two cubs are born weighing no more than 0·5 kg. each. These are not fully grown until they are ten years old.

Grizzlies vary enormously in colour, those in the north sometimes being creamy white, and elsewhere sometimes almost black. In spite of their great size, they can move surprisingly quickly, but have weak eyesight and indifferent hearing. They rely extensively on their sense of smell.

Canada Lynx (above)	Length, head and body	86 cm.
	Length of tail	10 cm.
	Shoulder height	58 cm.
Black Bear (below)	Length, head and body	170 cm.
	Length of tail	12 cm.
	Shoulder height	80 cm.

The Canada Lynx (family *Felidae*) is found in Alaska, Canada and the northern part of the United States as far south as Oregon.

These powerful, agile carnivores are nocturnal and are closely related to the Lynxes of Europe. Their food consists mainly of Rabbits and Snowshoe Hares, but many other mammals, including Deer, Foxes and Porcupines are caught.

One to four young (kittens), fully furred but blind at birth, are reared in a well-hidden den.

This species is subject to a periodic decline in numbers every ten years. This seems to coincide with a similar decrease in its principal food-source—the Snowshoe Hare. The numbers subsequently recover, but nowhere in the world are Lynxes as common as they once were.

The American Black Bear inhabits most of the United States and Canada, except northern Alaska and the Arctic regions. It is protected in National Parks, where it has greatly increased in numbers.

These Bears (family *Ursidae*) may be black, brown, cinnamon or silver, and the two or three cubs in a litter may be of different colours. A white race (the Kermode Bear) exists in British Columbia, and the Glacier Bear of south-east Alaska is blue-gray.

Cubs are born every two years during the winter, at which time the parents are in partial hibernation. Every sort of food is eaten, including tourists' offerings in National Parks. Feeding these Bears is unlawful and also unwise as they become aggressive when the supply stops. Like all Bears, they are unreliable as—unlike other carnivores—they give no warning at all of an impending attack.

Black Bears swim well and, unlike the Grizzly, are excellent climbers.

Polar Bear

Length, head and body	250 cm.
Shoulder height	160 cm.
Weight	410 kg.

Although this mammal is called the 'Polar' Bear, there are, in fact, no Polar Bears at the North Pole. Their habitat is the southern limit of the ice floes, where they constantly migrate to those areas where Seal—their principal diet—can be found.

This is by far the most carnivorous of Bears, and kills its prey by a blow from its gigantic front paws or by a bite through the head. Only occasionally does it come ashore and wander inland, and then rarely more than 150 kilometres from the sea. At these times it will eat grass and berries; but it is a selective feeder and does not often attack Musk Ox or Reindeer.

Polar Bears (family *Ursidae*) can swim for enormous distances and can run at about 40 k.p.h. (25 m.p.h.) Their fur, which in places is eight inches long, offers full protection against the severest cold and is even proof against water.

In early winter the female digs a den in the snow large enough for her to stand upright, and here she produces two cubs, which at birth are only 25 cm. long. They do not enter the water or leave their mother until they are eighteen months old. Polar Bears breed every other year and may live for thirty years or more.

Polar Bears are intensely inquisitive and quite unafraid of man. For this reason many have been easily killed in the past and are still quite needlessly hunted for so-called 'sport'. The world numbers of these Bears are fast declining, and the species is in some danger of extinction.

Coyote *(above)*

Length, head and body	90 cm.
Length of tail	30 cm.
Shoulder height	60 cm.

American Badger *(below)*

Length, head and body	70 cm.
Length of tail	12 cm.

It is said that these two animals form a hunting partnership, mutually assisting each other, although little is known of how this is arranged. Both are found in territory ranging from northern Alberta to Mexico, and are carnivores.

The Coyote (family *Canidae*) is, like the Badger, a predator of rodents and rabbits, and does much more good than harm to the interests of human beings. Yet both animals are destroyed by ranchers and farmers who, like many other people, seem to be unaware of the importance of predators in nature.

Coyotes hunt singly or in small packs, and can travel at 60 k.p.h. (45 m.p.h.). The nocturnal call of the Coyote can be heard for miles across the prairie.

Coyotes mate for life and produce each year one litter of from five to ten pups. These are raised in a den and fed by both parents. They are extremely intelligent and adaptable animals, and have thus survived in spite of changes to their habitat and centuries of persecution.

The American Badger (family *Mustelidae*) is a remarkable digger, able to dig fast enough to hide itself from an enemy or to catch rodents before they can escape. It also eats rabbits, large insects, birds and their eggs, and is quite capable of killing and eating venomous snakes. It is nocturnal, inhabiting open country and prairie.

Usually two young are born in a den in a burrow lined with grass. Each adult Badger requires a territory of about 1500 metres in diameter. Few animals will attack a Badger, which is more than a match for any dog—or even an unarmed man.

Timber Wolf
(Gray Wolf)

Length, head and body	*120 cm.*
Length of tail	*40 cm.*
Shoulder height	*80 cm.*

Wolves (family *Canidae*) are found in North America, Asia and Europe, but are everywhere becoming scarcer. They are animals of the wild places—pine forests, prairie or steppe. Because Wolves sometimes prey on cattle, man has gradually exterminated them, and by cultivating wild territory has destroyed much of their habitat. This is a great pity because the Wolf, which preys largely on sick, aged or weak animals, performs a most necessary function.

In North America, Wolves are now found chiefly in the Canadian Rockies, in Alaska and in a few isolated areas of the United States. The Red Wolf, a separate species, is now rather rare but remnants remain in Texas and Louisiana.

Wolves live in family groups or small packs which have an interesting social structure. They are remarkably affectionate to one another and are believed to mate for life. Both male and female are excellent parents.

Four or five cubs, born blind, constitute the average litter which may be of mixed colours. They are kept in a den which is often a hole deliberately excavated by the Wolves themselves. A pack consists normally of fewer than fifteen animals, and these hunt by wearing-down prey rather than by speed. Apparently tireless, trotting Wolves can cover as many as 90 kilometres in a night.

Although small animals such as rodents are eaten, the preferred prey consists of deer of all sizes. Wolves very rarely attack human beings, and only extreme hunger will drive them to do so.

The Wolves of Alaska and the Mackenzie River are much paler and very much larger than any others.

32

Bobcat (Bay Lynx)

Length, head and body   82 cm.
Length of tail   16 cm.

Usually smaller than the Canada Lynx, the Bobcat differs also in having a tawnier, shorter coat more positively marked, shorter ear tufts and smaller feet. Although the range of the two species overlaps, the Bobcat is not found north of southern Canada, but is found throughout the United States as far south as central Mexico.

This solitary animal (family *Felidae*) is seldom seen, and inhabits both swampland and woodland. It has no permanent home, except in the breeding season, and has a territory of about sixty square kilometres which it marks by leaving characteristic scratches on trees.

Chiefly nocturnal, the Bobcat will cover as many as forty kilometres in a night, preying on rabbits, birds and occasionally deer. It does not suffer from the same periodic decline in numbers as the Lynx, as it is not so dependent on the supply of Snowshoe Hares as a source of food.

Coyotes, Foxes and even Owls will kill Bobcat kittens, and man has persecuted this species for centuries. The Bobcat has, however, learned to survive more effectively than the Lynx, and the fact that its fur is not so highly prized by trappers may also contribute to its survival.

Normally there is one litter of three or four kittens a year, but some female Bobcats (which like all wildcats are smaller than the male) produce two litters. These kittens are born blind and, like most wildcats, with spotted fur.

Silent at other times of the year, Bobcats yowl and caterwaul at mating time (March). They have marvellous eyesight and hearing, climb and swim well and, in the wild, live for about ten years.

Cougar

Length, head and body 170 cm.
Length of tail 80 cm.

Cougar, Puma, Mountain Lion, Painter or Catamount—these are all different names for the same animal, which ranges throughout both North and South America from British Columbia to Tierra del Fuego. This is the greatest range of any mammal in the New World.

The Great Cats (those that roar) are the Lion, Tiger, Leopard, Snow Leopard and Jaguar; all are placed in the genus *Panthera* (family *Felidae*). The other lesser Cats (except the Cheetah) are placed in the genus *Felis,* and of these the Cougar is the largest.

Because of the varying habitats occupied by the Cougar, the size and colour varies. Those which live in the north are large and those from tropical climates smaller and darker. The principal food is deer—one animal the size of a Mule Deer being the average kill each week. Other foods include rodents, large and small. Prey is caught by stalking it—not by chasing like a Cheetah or lying in wait like a Leopard. Cougars will return to a kill but generally they prefer fresh-killed meat.

Three cubs, spotted, blind and very small, constitute the average litter and they are born in a well-concealed den at any time of the year. They are exceptionally playful and are raised by the mother alone, staying with her until they are about two years old. The life span is up to twenty years.

Usually silent, at mating time Cougars yowl, scream and even whistle. When at ease they purr. Instances of man-eating are very rare, only occurring when the Cougar is intensely hungry, wounded or suffering from rabies.

Pronghorn (Buck)

Length, head and body	*136 cm.*
Shoulder height	*94 cm.*
Horns	*25 cm.*

The Pronghorn is the only member of the family *Antilocapridae* and is strictly neither an antelope nor a deer. It is the only survivor of a group of the order *Artiodactyla* that developed in prehistoric times. The horns of both sexes have a permanent bony core upon which a sheath of hard, fused hair grows each year and which is shed after the breeding season.

Pronghorns inhabit prairie and desert from Saskatchewan to Mexico, but only in isolated 'pockets' and not as a continuous population. They are hunted by Wolves and Coyotes, Cougars and Bobcats—and by Man, but they are able to survive because of their wariness and by using their immense speed, which can be as much as 65 k.p.h.

Almost any sort of vegetation, including cactus, is eaten, and in snow the front feet are used for digging for food. As with other desert animals, a regular supply of water is not essential. A woolly undercoat, covered by an outer coat of harsh, brittle hair protects the Pronghorn against the cold. In summer heat, the outer coat can be raised or lowered by muscles in the skin, and thus the body temperature is kept constant. Two patches of white hair on the rump are also controlled in this way.

Twin calves, born and hidden some ninety metres apart, are raised by the mother on milk which is exceptionally rich. At four days old they can run faster than a man.

Pronghorns have enormous eyes which give them very long sight and a very wide angle of vision. In many areas they are in some danger of extinction.

Wapiti (above)	Length, head and body	250 cm.
	Length of tail	20 cm.
	Shoulder height	145 cm.

*Caribou (below)	Length, head and body	200 cm. ⎫ very
	Length of tail	15 cm. ⎬ variable
	Shoulder height	130 cm. ⎭

'Wapiti' is the Shawnee Indian's word for an animal which is sometimes referred to as an Elk in North America. Similarly, the Alonquian Indians used the word 'Caribou' which means 'shoveller', to describe the Reindeer and its habit of scraping in snow for food.

Wapiti (family *Cervidae*) are closely related to the Red Deer of Europe and Asia. They are bigger than European Deer and have much bigger antlers. They live in large herds, inhabiting mountain meadowland in summer and wooded valleys in winter. Once numerous, they are now found only in the Rocky Mountains and from British Columbia south to central California. Wolves and Cougars are their principal enemies other than Man, who has killed thousands as trophies.

Calves are usually single and are speckled with white.

Caribou collect in huge migratory herds all round the Arctic Circle, in Siberia and Lapland as well as in northern Canada. Both males and females carry antlers—the only members of the family *Cervidae* to do so. Those of the males are huge and of fantastic shapes. There is great variety in colour, and some races, such as the Peary Caribou, are almost white.

In North America, Caribou are not found further south than Lake Superior. They form a very important part of the economy of the Eskimos who, in Alaska, have imported the more easily domesticated European Reindeer. Thus considerable interbreeding between races has occurred. Since 1930, the herds have been greatly reduced.

Single calves, not spotted like most other deer, are born in summer; in a few hours they can run several miles.

* *See also in 'European Mammals', to be published shortly in this series.*

Moose

Length, head and body	275 cm.
Shoulder height	185 cm.
Record antler spread	196 cm.

Moose are the largest of the family *Cervidae,* bulls bearing the heaviest antlers of all deer, and with legs so long that they have to kneel down to graze. They are almost entirely browsers, living on leaves and branches of such trees as willow or on water plants. When gathering the latter, they frequently submerge completely. A full-grown Moose requires about 25 kg. of food a day. Moose inhabit wooded and marshy areas, are strong swimmers with a highly-developed sense of smell and hearing, but have poor eye-sight.

In North America, Moose range from Maine through most of Canada to Alaska and south to northern Colorado. In Europe, where they are called Elk, they are found in small numbers in Norway and Sweden, more abundantly in Russia and Siberia, and in Asia in Manchuria and Mongolia. The numbers in North America are recovering after being somewhat depleted.

Moose are normally solitary animals, but at breeding time bulls remain with the cow until the calf is ten days old. Calves stay with their mother for a year, until the next calf is born. They are not spotted and are reddish in colour; twins or triplets only occur rarely. Like the bellowing adults at mating time, calves are rather noisy, frequently whimpering and grunting.

Bulls shed their huge antlers in December, and in April begin to grow new ones. Until July the antlers are extremely sensitive and are covered with a thin skin which has the appearance of velvet. This skin then peels off, revealing the hardened antler beneath.

White-tailed Deer (above)

Mule Deer (below)

BOTH
- Length, head and body   180 cm.
- Length of tail   30 cm.
- Shoulder height   90 cm.

These two rather similar species (family *Cervidae*) are most easily distinguished by their tails and by the type of antlers carried by the bucks. Mule Deer are found in western Canada and the western United States, as far south as northern Mexico. Their tails are white, black-tipped and rounded, and their antlers branch into two parts. The tail of the White-Tail, on the other hand, is broad and edged with white, and the antlers have one main 'beam' with minor branches. White-Tails are found in varying forms in southern Canada, all over the United States and as far south as northern South America.

Neither species lives in herds and, although Mule Deer are found in deserts, the usual habitat is wooded country with enough cover to provide hiding places. In winter, when they have longer, much grayer coats, they may form small herds whenever food is plentiful. Although many starve in winter, these deer are very abundant—an estimated population of five million animals over the whole range.

Some races of White-Tail are very small and are known as Key Deer. They have tiny hoofs, the size of a man's thumbnail, and are in some danger of extinction.

Young White-Tails produce single fawns, but otherwise both species produce families of two, three or four. These are spotted, scentless, and are hidden in separate places by the mother. She feeds them on very rich milk and they are weaned in six weeks.

Food consists of a wide variety of vegetation, and these deer are both grazers (grass-eaters) and browsers (leaf-eaters).

Bison

Bull:	Length, head and body	350 cm.
	Length of tail	60 cm.
	Shoulder height	190 cm.
	Weight	900 kg.
Cows considerably smaller.		

This is the largest mammal in the New World and, before the advent of European settlers, wandered over the North American prairies in herds amounting in all to fifty million animals. By 1889, this great number had been reduced to a total of 541. They were shot for food, particularly for the workers building the railways, and also for sport. Today, thanks to protection, Bison live in National Parks—about six thousand in the United States and probably twenty-five thousand in Canada.

Bison (family *Bovidae*) can move remarkably quickly, and are unreliable and dangerous animals. Herds are led by a cow, except at mating-time when a bull takes over. Both sexes have horns and all Bison are fond of wallowing in mud and rolling in huge dust-baths, presumably to rid themselves of ticks and of irritation caused by moulting.

North American Bison are grazers, feeding in the early morning and evening. Life expectancy is about fifteen years in the wild, although in captivity they do not usually live so long. They have poor eye-sight, but a good sense of smell and hearing.

As with other members of the family *Bovidae,* bulls fight savagely for the cows at mating-time, but later form separate all-male herds. A single golden-yellow calf (rarely twins) is born between April and June in a place apart from the herd. Calves are protected by the cow and often by the bull and the rest of the herd also. Cows feed their calves for nearly a year and protect them for up to three years, after which they themselves can breed.

Musk Ox

Length, head and body	230 cm.
Length of tail	10 cm.
Shoulder height	160 cm.
Weight	400 kg.

Once, in prehistoric times, an inhabitant of Europe (including Britain), Siberia and the United States, the Musk Ox is now restricted to tundra and snowfields in northern Canada and Greenland. This very ancient species, placed in a genus *Ovibus* (family *Bovidae*) by itself, lies in the scheme of things somewhere between the cattle and the sheep.

Huge splayed feet enable it to move readily (and surprisingly quickly, if necessary) across snow. The fur, consisting of a fine woolly undercoat and coarser outer hair, protects against both rain and snow in winter and against the attacks of mosquitoes (which abound in its habitat) in summer.

Musk Ox are gregarious, forming fairly large herds, usually widely spaced, which provide defensive rings against the attacks of such predators as Wolves or Grizzlies. Young animals remain within the ring, while the adults present a solid outer circle. They never retreat.

The introduction of firearms proved disastrous to the Musk Ox population, their massed groups presenting too easy a target. Now protected in Canada, there are some ten thousand of them left. They have excellent eye-sight, with special pupils which shield their eyes from the glare of the snow. Their name derives from the musky smell of their fur. Food consists of vegetation, bark, moss and lichens for which, like Caribou, they dig through deep snow.

The single calf is kept warm and dry under the mother's dense 'skirt' of hair.

This is a very ancient species, living specimens being almost identical with the prehistoric form.

| **Rocky Mountain** | Length, head and body | 150 cm. |
| **Goat** *(above)* | Length of tail | 13 cm. |

| **Bighorn Sheep** | Length, head and body | 180 cm. |
| *(below)* | Shoulder height | 100 cm. |

High in the Rocky Mountains above the tree line lives the Rocky Mountain Goat (family *Bovidae*), found also in mountains in Alaska, Montana and south to northern Oregon. This is not a true goat—but what is known as a 'goat-antelope', related to the Chamois of Europe.

Specially adapted hoofs with a sharp rim and padded centre enable this animal to maintain a foothold on precipitous rocks and narrow ledges. In such a habitat it has to be both browser and grazer, picking up whatever it can. It is an exceptional climber and jumper, and for this reason has few enemies; nor is it prized as a trophy. Avalanches probably cause more casualties among these Goats than predators such as Eagles and Cougars.

One or two kids are born in May or June, and mature rapidly.

Lower down on the mountains, from British Columbia to Alberta and south to New Mexico, lives the magnificently horned Bighorn Sheep (family *Bovidae*). Much sought after as a big game trophy, it is by no means as plentiful now as it once was.

Bighorns are noted for the noisy and spectacular battles between the rams at breeding-time. They will continue to charge at each other, head to head, for as long as two hours at a time. In spite of this, there are relatively few fatalities.

Like all wild sheep (as opposed to domestic sheep), Bighorns do not grow thick woolly coats in spite of their habitat. They are principally grazers, whose lambs (born singly) can very soon climb among crags and precipices.

INDEX

Page 4   Alaskan Pika
Canadian Porcupine

6   Snowshoe Hare
American Marten

8   Prairie Dog
Cottontail Rabbit

10   North American Flying Squirrel
American Mink

12   Eastern Chipmunk
White-footed Mouse

14   Fox Squirrel
Eastern Gray Fox

16   Beaver
Musk Rat

18   Fisher
Striped Skunk

20   Douglas Squirrel (Chickaree)
Cacomistle (Ring-tailed Cat)

22   Raccoon
Opossum

24   Grizzly Bear

26   Canada Lynx
Black Bear

28   Polar Bear

30   Coyote : American Badger

32   Timber Wolf
(Gray Wolf)

34   Bobcat (Bay Lynx)

36   Cougar

38   Pronghorn (Buck)

40   Wapiti
Caribou

42   Moose

44   White-tailed Deer : Mule Deer

46   Bison

48   Musk Ox

50   Rocky Mountain Goat : Bighorn Sheep